JEHOVAH-RAPHA

The Lord Who Heals

Chaplain Tonya C. Smith

JEHOVAH-RAPHA
The Lord Who Heals
by Chaplain Tonya C. Smith
https://www.facebook.com/LADYT4CHRIST
Email: ChaplainTCSmith@gmail.com

Cover and interior design by DJM Ministries

ISBN-13: 978-1986920803
ISBN-10:1986920801

DEDICATED

TO GOD THE Father, to Jesus Christ who died for the remission of my sins, and to the Holy Spirit that dwells on the inside and illuminates to the outer appearance.

To my grandparents that all gained their angel wings. To my parents my father that gained his angel wings on July 18, 2015, Charles Daniel Smith Sr. He was a great husband, father, grandfather, great grandfather, provider for his family. The first and only man that I can say I truly loved unconditionally. When he passed a part of me passed also. This book is dedicated to my mother, my BFF, my prayer partner, my greatest supporter, Virginia. She is a great mother, grandmother, great grandmother. I'm the youngest of their four children.

To my four children LaTonya and her husband Elijah, Tiffany, Jasmine and Tyler. You sacrificed so much as I have walked in my God ordained ministry. I thank God for each one of you. I did not do everything perfectly, but you all have helped me to be the woman of God that I am. I thank you for not giving up on me.

To my two grandchildren Elijah and Aniyah. You make me smile when it's just not one of those days of feeling happy. My household has been my support system since day one.

They have always given me the love and support that I have always needed throughout the years to accomplish all that God has ordained for my life. I have dedicated my life to ministering and praying for others ever since I could remember and I'm glad about it. My prayer for this book is that it helps people across the world to pray one for another.

TABLE OF CONTENTS

INTRODUCTION:
Jehovah-Rapha

ALLOW ME JUST a moment to explain the meaning of "Jehovah-Rapha". "Jehovah means the external one, the ever living one and the self- existing one. "Rapha" is the Hebrew word for "heal". Therefore, "Jehovah-Rapha" can be translated as "I am the Lord your physician", or "I am the Lord your Healer".

The bible says in Proverbs 4:20, "My son, attend to my words, incline thine ear into my sayings. Let them not depart from thine eyes; keep them in the midst of thine heart. For they are life to those that finds them, and health (or medicine) to all their flesh.' God's word is life and health to your flesh.

If you have been diagnosed with a serious illness, do not lose hope. I have selected many scriptures from the bible which speaks of healing and recovery. God's word is supernatural. I hope they will help you fight as much as they have been a constant source of encouragement, support, strength, life, medicine and joy to me whole being.

What Does The Word Heal Mean?

The word "Heal" means to make healthy, whole, or sound. It means to restore to health. It means to be free from ailments. It means to bring to an end or conclusion, as conflicts between people or groups, usually with the strong implications of restoring form amity.

It means to settle and it means to reconcile. Furthermore, it means to be free from evil, to cleanse or to purify. It means to heal the soul, or to effect a cure such as a wound or broken bone.

It also refers to curing or curative, prescribed or helping to heal. It means growing sound, getting well or mending. It refers to the act or process of regaining health.

CHAPTER 1:
Does God Heal Today

I HAVE HEARD people say, "it's God's will" or "I'll just leave it up to God" when faced with a serious illness or tragedy. Don't fall into that trap. God wants us to pray to him for help. In Luke 18:1:

> "Jesus told his disciples that they should always pray and not give up and then Jesus asked will not God bring about justice for his chosen ones, who cry out to him day and night?"

Pray to God from your heart for healing. Don't stop. Don't give up. God wants us to ask him for help. He loves us. Over twenty percent of the gospel is about the healing ministry of Jesus Christ.

Jesus taught his disciples how to pray and heal. He sent them to carry on his work. Wouldn't Jesus want his followers to pray for healing today? Many spiritual writers have defined the call of healing so narrowly that some people feel they don't qualify. But today a new awakening in faith has made us realize we are not only called into healing for ourselves but also in various degrees into healing each other.

The bible gives us some directions on how to pray for healing. For example, in James 5:14-15 we are told,

> *"is any one of you sick? He should call elders of the church to pray over him and anoint him with oil in the name of the Lord. And the prayer offered in faith will make the sick person well; the Lord will raise him up. If he has sinned, he will be forgiven.*

In James 5:16 we are asked to,

> *"Confess your sins to each other and pray for each other so that you may be healed and then told that the prayer of a righteous man is powerful and effective.*

In Mark 11:23-25,

"Jesus further instructs to forgive when we pray "I tell you the truth if anyone says to this mountain, Go, throw yourself into the sea, and does not doubt in his heart but believes that what he says will happen, it will be done for hm. Therefore, I tell you whatever you ask for in prayer believe that you have received it and it will be yours. And when you stand praying if you hold anything against anyone forgive him so that your Father in Heaven may forgive you your sins".

Only someone facing or sharing a serious sickness, pain or tragedy knows how hard it is. They know how hard it is to cope with the fear and uncertainty. They know how absurd it sounds when someone first tells them to "keep a positive attitude". They know how terrifying it is when the doubt comes. They know how hard it is to throw a mountain into the sea.

But remember what Jesus told us in Matthew 17:19-20 when he said,

"I tell you the truth, if you have faith as small as a mustard seed, you can say to this mountain, move from here to there and t will move, nothing will be impossible for you".

Faith as small as a mustard seed sounds a little like hope to me and that's a good start.

CHAPTER 2:
Six Things To Contemplate And Act On

First is prayer it's just common sense that you're not likely to get something unless you ask for it. Jesus told his disciples to pray night and day and not to give up. He also told us to have the elders of the church pray for us. Scripture references James 5:14-15; Luke 18:1-7; James 5:16 and Matthew 18:19-20.

Second if faith while a great amount of faith is not required for God to heal, it certainly can't hurt. Jesus was unable to do miracles in his hometown because of the lack of faith but he was still able to heal sick people! With faith Jesus tells us that "nothing will be impossible for you". Scripture references Mark 6:1-6 and Matthew 17:19.

Third is love and forgiveness. There is no question that God wants us to love and forgive each other. Love is God's commandment. Love is healing. Scripture references John 15:12-14; Hebrews 13:1-2; Isaiah 58:7-8, 1 Corinthians 13:4-7; Mark 11:23-25, Proverbs 15:30; Proverbs 12:18 and Proverbs 16:24

Fourth is God's protection there are forces of evil that you may need protection from. Ask God for protection. Scripture reference Ephesians 6:11-13.

Fifth is good medical care. God works his miracles in many ways and through many people. Today's medical community has a lot to offer and with God's grace can save your life. Scripture reference Luke 5:31.

Six is a healthy diet. There are many references in the bible about what we should and shouldn't eat. Today's is the "Mediterranean Diet" follow the biblical reference Ezekiel 47:12.

CHAPTER 3:
Forty Scriptures On Healing

ROMANS 10 TELLS us that faith comes from hearing and hearing from the word of Christ. To help us believe God for healing ourselves, our friends and our families it helps to have a good grasp of the Scriptures concerning healing. These Scriptures are small enough to be written on a business card sized bit of paper, carried around and memorized.

1. *(Exodus 15:26 NKJV) and said, "If you diligently heed the voice of the LORD your God and do what is right in His sight, give ear*

to His commandments and keep all His statutes, I will put none of the diseases on you which I have brought on the Egyptians. For I am the LORD who heals you."

2. *(Deuteronomy 32:39 NKJV) 'Now see that I, even I, am He, and there is no God besides Me; I kill, and I make alive; I wound, and I heal; Nor is there any who can deliver from My hand.*

3. *(2 Chronicles 7:14 NKJV) "If My people who are called by My name will humble themselves, and pray and seek My face, and turn from their wicked ways, then I will hear from heaven, and will forgive their sin and heal their land.*

4. *(Psalms 30:2 NKJV) O LORD my God, I cried out to You, And You healed me.*

5. *(Psalms 6:2 NKJV) Have mercy on me, O LORD, for I am weak; O LORD, heal me, for my bones are troubled.*

6. *(Psalms 103:1-4 NKJV) Bless the LORD, O my soul; And all that is within me, bless His holy name! {2} Bless the LORD, O my soul, and forget not all His benefits: {3} Who forgives all your iniquities, who heals all your diseases, {4} Who redeems your life*

from destruction, who crowns you with lovingkindness and tender mercies.

7. *(Psalms 107:20 NKJV) He sent His word and healed them, And delivered them from their destructions.*

8. *(Psalms 147:3 NKJV) He heals the brokenhearted and binds up their wounds.*

9. *(Proverbs 3:7-8 NKJV) Do not be wise in your own eyes; Fear the LORD and depart from evil. {8} It will be health to your flesh, And strength to your bones.*

10. *(Proverbs 4:20-22 NKJV) My son, give attention to my words; Incline your ear to my sayings. {21} Do not let them depart from your eyes; Keep them in the midst of your heart; {22} For they are life to those who find them, And health to all their flesh.*

11. *(Isaiah 53:5 NKJV) But He was wounded for our transgressions, He was bruised for our iniquities; The chastisement for our peace was upon Him, And by His stripes we are healed.*

12. *(Isaiah 58:8 NKJV) Then your light shall break forth like the morning, your healing shall spring forth speedily, and your*

righteousness shall go before you; The glory of the LORD shall be your rear guard.

13. *(Isaiah 61:1 NKJV)* "*The Spirit of the Lord GOD is upon Me, Because the LORD has anointed Me To preach good tidings to the poor; He has sent Me to heal the brokenhearted, to proclaim liberty to the captives, And the opening of the prison to those who are bound.*

14. *(Jeremiah 3:22 NKJV)* "*Return, you backsliding children, And I will heal your backslidings." "Indeed, we do come to You, For You are the LORD our God.*

15. *(Jeremiah 17:14 NKJV) Heal me, O LORD, and I shall be healed; Save me, and I shall be saved, For You are my praise.*

16. *(Jeremiah 30:17 NKJV) For I will restore health to you and heal you of your wounds,' says the LORD, 'Because they called you an outcast saying: "This is Zion; No one seeks her."'*

17. *(Jeremiah 33:6 NKJV) 'Behold, I will bring it health and healing; I will heal them and reveal to them the abundance of peace and truth.*

18. *(Hosea 6:1 NKJV) Come, and let us return to the LORD; For He has torn, but He will heal us; He has stricken, but He will bind us up.*

19. *(Hosea 14:4 NKJV) "I will heal their backsliding, I will love them freely, For My anger has turned away from him.*

20. *(Malachi 4:2 NKJV) But to you who fear My Name the Sun of Righteousness shall arise with healing in His wings; And you shall go out and grow fat like stall-fed calves.*

21. *(Matthew 4:23 NKJV) And Jesus went about all Galilee, teaching in their synagogues, preaching the gospel of the kingdom, and healing all kinds of sickness and all kinds of disease among the people.*

22. *(Matthew 8:13 NKJV) Then Jesus said to the centurion, "Go your way; and as you have believed, so let it be done for you." And his servant was healed that same hour.*

23. *(Matthew 8:16 NKJV) When evening had come, they brought to Him many who were demon-possessed. And He cast out the spirits with a word, and healed all who were sick.*

24. *(Matthew 9:35 NKJV) Then Jesus went about all the cities and villages, teaching in their synagogues, preaching the gospel of the kingdom, and healing every sickness and every disease among the people.*

25. *(Matthew 10:1 NKJV) And when He had called His twelve disciples to Him, He gave them power over unclean spirits, to cast them out, and to heal all kinds of sickness and all kinds of disease.*

26. *(Matthew 10:8 NKJV) "Heal the sick, cleanse the lepers, raise the dead, cast out demons. Freely you have received, freely give.*

27. *(Matthew 12:22 NKJV) Then one was brought to Him who was demon-possessed, blind and mute; and He healed him, so that the blind and mute man both spoke and saw.*

28. *(Matthew 14:14 NKJV) And when Jesus went out He saw a great multitude; and He was moved with compassion for them, and healed their sick.*

29. *(Luke 6:19 NKJV) And the whole multitude sought to touch Him, for power went out from Him and healed them all.*

30. *(Luke 9:6 NKJV) So they departed and went through the towns, preaching the gospel and healing everywhere. (The twelve are sent out).*

31. *(Luke 10:8-9 NKJV) "Whatever city you enter, and they receive you, eat such things as are set before you. {9} "And heal the sick there, and say to them, 'The kingdom of God has come near to you.' (The seventy are sent out)*

32. *(Luke 17:15 NKJV) And one of them, when he saw that he was healed, returned, and with a loud voice glorified God, (The story of the ten lepers).*

33. *(Acts 3:12 NKJV) So when Peter saw it, he responded to the people: "Men of Israel, why do you marvel at this? Or why look so intently at us, as though by our own power or godliness we had made this man walk?*

34. *(Healing of the lame man at the Gate Beautiful) (Acts 4:29-31 NKJV) "Now, Lord, look on their threats, and grant to Your servants that with all boldness they may speak Your word, {30} "by stretching out Your hand to heal, and that signs and wonders may be done through the name of Your Holy Servant Jesus." {31}*

And when they had prayed, the place where they were assembled
together was shaken; and they were all filled with the Holy Spirit,
and they spoke the word of God with boldness.

35. *(1 Corinthians 12:9 NKJV) to another faith by the same Spirit,*
    to another gift of healings by the same Spirit.

36. *(James 5:14-16 NKJV) Is anyone among you sick? Let him call*
    for the elders of the church, and let them pray over him, anointing
    him with oil in the name of the Lord. {15} And the prayer of
    faith will save the sick, and the Lord will raise him up. And if he
    has committed sins, he will be forgiven. {16} Confess your
    trespasses to one another, and pray for one another, that you may
    be healed. The effective, fervent prayer of a righteous man avails
    much.

37. *(Revelation 22:2 NKJV) In the middle of its street, and on either*
    side of the river, was the tree of life, which bore twelve fruits, each
    tree yielding its fruit every month. The leaves of the tree were for the
    healing of the nations.

38. *(Luke 8:47 NKJV) Now when the woman saw that she was not*
    hidden, she came trembling; and falling down before Him, she

declared to Him in the presence of all the people the reason she had

touched Him and how she was healed immediately.

39. *(Luke 8:48 NKJV) And He said to her, "Daughter, be of good*

    cheer; your faith has made you well. Go in peace.".

40. *(Luke 5:17 NKJV) Now it happened on a certain day, as He*

    was teaching, that there were Pharisees and teachers of the law

    sitting by, who had come out of every town of Galilee, Judea, and

    Jerusalem. And the power of the Lord was present to heal them.

CHAPTER 4:
Prayer For Healing The Sick

Dear God,

You are the one I turn to for help in moments of weakness and times of need. I ask you to be with your servant in this illness. Psalm 107:20 says that you send out your Word and heal. So then, please send your healing Word to your servant. In the name of Jesus, drive out all infirmity and sickness from his body.

Oh God, I ask you to turn this weakness into strength, this suffering into compassion, sorrow into joy, and pain into comfort for others. May your servant trust in your goodness and hope in your faithfulness, even in the middle of this suffering. Let him be filled with patience and joy in your presence as he waits for your healing touch.

Please restore your servant to full health, dear Father. Remove all fear and doubt from his heart by the power of your Holy Spirit, and may you, Lord, be glorified through his life. As you heal and renew your servant oh Lord, may he bless and praise you.

All of this, I pray in the name of Jesus Christ.

AMEN.

CHAPTER 5:
Prayer For A Sick Friend

Dear God,

You know *[name of friend or family member]* so much better than I do. You know his/her sickness and the burden he carries. You also know his heart. Lord, I ask you to be with my friend now as you work in his life.

Lord, let your will be done in *[name of friend or family member]* life. If there is a sin that needs to be confessed and forgiven, please help him to see his need and confess.

Lord, I pray for *[name of friend or family member]* just as your Word tells me to pray, for healing. I believe you hear this earnest prayer from my heart and that it is powerful because of your promise. I have faith in you, Lord, to heal *[name of friend or family member]*, but I also trust in the plan you have for *[name of friend or family member]*.

Lord, I don't always understand your ways. I don't know why *[name of friend or family member]* must suffer, but I trust you. I ask that you look with mercy and grace toward *[name of friend or family member]*. Nourish his spirit and soul in this time of suffering and comfort *[name of friend or family member]* with your presence.

Let *[name of friend or family member]* know you are there with him/her through this difficulty. Give him/her strength. And may you, through this difficulty, be glorified in his life and in mine.

AMEN.

CHAPTER 6:
Why Doesn't God Heal Everyone?

ONE OF THE names of God is Jehovah-Rapha, "the Lord who heals." In Exodus 15:26, God declares that he is the healer of his people. The passage refers specifically to healing from physical disease. He said,

> *"If you will listen carefully to the voice of the Lord your God and do what is right in his sight, obeying his commands and keeping all his decrees, then I will not*

make you suffer any of the diseases I sent on the
Egyptians; for I am the Lord who heals you." (NLT)

The Bible records a considerable number of physical healing accounts in the Old Testament. Likewise, in the ministry of Jesus and his disciples, healing miracles are prominently highlighted. And throughout the ages of church history, believers have continued to testify of God's power to divinely heal the sick.

So, if God by his own nature declares himself Healer, why doesn't God heal everyone?

Why did God use Paul to heal the father of Publius who was ill with fever and dysentery, as well as many other sick people, yet not his beloved disciple Timothy who suffered from frequent stomach illnesses?

Eight Reasons Why
God Doesn't Heal Everyone

1.   God's Sovereignty

Perhaps you are suffering from a sickness right now. You've prayed every healing Bible verse you know, and still, you're left wondering, *why won't God heal me?* Maybe you've recently lost a loved one to cancer or some other terrible disease. It's only natural to ask the question: *Why does God heal some people but not others?*

The quick and obvious answer to the question rests in God's sovereignty. God is in control and ultimately, he knows what's best for his creations. While this is certainly true, there are several clear-cut reasons given in Scripture to further explain why God may not heal.

Now, before we dive in, I want to admit something: I don't fully understand all the reasons God does not heal. I have struggled with my own personal "thorn in the flesh" for years. I'm referring to 2 Corinthians 12:8-9, where the Apostle Paul stated:

> *Three different times I begged the Lord to take it away. Each time he said, "My grace is all you need. My power works best in weakness." So now I am glad to boast about my weaknesses, so that the power of Christ can work through me. (NLT)*

Like Paul, I pleaded (in my case for years) for relief, for healing. Eventually, like the apostle, I resolved in my weakness to live in the sufficiency of God's grace.

During my earnest quest for answers about healing, I was fortunate to learn a few things. And so, I will pass those on to you.

2. *Unconfessed Sin*

We'll cut to the chase with this first one: sometimes sickness is the result of unconfessed sin. I know, I didn't like this answer either, but it's right there in Scripture:

Confess your sins to each other and pray for each other so that you may be healed. The earnest prayer of a righteous person has great power and produces wonderful results. (James 5:16, NLT)

I want to stress that sickness is not *always* the direct result of sin in someone's life, but pain and disease are part of this fallen, cursed world in which we currently live.

We must be careful not to blame every sickness on sin, but we must also realize it is one possible reason. Thus, a good place to begin if you've come to the Lord for healing is to search your heart and confess your sins.

3. Lack of Faith

When Jesus healed the sick, on many occasions he made this statement: "Your faith has made you well." In Matthew 9:20-22, Jesus healed the woman who had suffered for many years with constant bleeding:

Just then a woman who had suffered for twelve years with constant bleeding came up behind him. She touched the fringe of his robe, for she thought, "If I can just touch his robe, I will be healed."

Jesus turned around, and when he saw her he said, "Daughter, be encouraged! Your faith has made you well." And the woman was healed at that moment. (NLT)

Here are a few more biblical examples of healing in response to faith:

> *Matthew 9:28–29; Mark 2:5, Luke 17:19; Acts 3:16; James 5:14–16.*

Apparently, there is an important link between faith and healing. Given the multitude of Scriptures connecting faith to healing, we must conclude that *sometimes* healing does not occur because of a lack of faith, or better, the pleasing kind of faith that God honors. Again, we must be careful not to assume every time someone isn't healed the reason is a lack of faith.

4.   *Failure To Ask*

If we don't ask and earnestly desire to be healed, God won't answer. When Jesus saw a lame man, who had been sick for 38 years he asked, "Would you like to get well?" That may seem like an odd question from Jesus, but immediately the man gave excuses:

> *"I can't, sir," he said, "for I have no one to put me into the pool when the water bubbles up. Someone else always gets there ahead of me." (John 5:6-7, NLT)*

Jesus looked into the man's heart and saw his reluctance to be healed.

Maybe you know someone who is addicted to stress or crisis. They don't know how to behave without turmoil in their life, and so they begin to orchestrate their own atmosphere of chaos. Similarly, some people may not want to be healed because they've linked their personal identity so closely with their illness. These individuals may fear the unknown aspects of life beyond their sickness, or crave the attention that the affliction provides.

James 4:2 plainly states, "You do not have, because you do not ask." (ESV)

5. *Need For Deliverance*

Scripture also indicates that *some* illnesses are caused by spiritual or demonic influences.

> *And you know that God anointed Jesus of Nazareth with the Holy Spirit and with power. Then Jesus went around doing good and healing all who were oppressed by the devil, for God was with him. (Acts 10:38, NLT)*

In Luke 13, Jesus healed a woman crippled by an evil spirit:

> *One Sabbath day as Jesus was teaching in a synagogue, he saw a woman who had been crippled by an evil spirit. She had been bent double for eighteen years and was unable to stand up straight. When Jesus saw her, he called her over and said, "Dear woman, you are healed of*

your sickness!" Then he touched her, and instantly she could stand straight. How she praised God! (Luke 13:10-13)

Even Paul called his thorn in the flesh a "messenger from Satan":

...even though I have received such wonderful revelations from God. So, to keep me from becoming proud, I was given a thorn in my flesh, a messenger from Satan to torment me and keep me from becoming proud. (2 Corinthians 12:7, NLT)

So, there are times when a demonic or spiritual cause must be addressed before healing can occur.

6. *A Higher Purpose*

C.S. Lewis wrote in his book, *The Problem of Pain*: "God whispers to us in our pleasures, speaks in our conscience, but shouts in our pain, it is his megaphone to rouse a deaf world."

We may not understand it at the time, but sometimes God desires to do more than simply heal our physical bodies. Often, in his infinite wisdom, God will use physical suffering to develop our character and produce spiritual growth in us.

I've discovered, but only through looking back on my life, that God had a higher purpose for letting me struggle for years with a painful disability. Rather than healing me, God used the trial to redirect me, first, toward a desperate dependence on him, and second, to the path of purpose and destiny he had planned for my life. He knew where I would be most productive and fulfilled serving him, and he knew the path it would take to get me there.

I'm not suggesting that you ever stop praying for healing, but also ask God to show you the higher plan or better purpose he may be accomplishing through your pain.

7. *God's Glory*

Sometimes when we pray for healing, our situation goes from bad to worse. When this happens, it's possible that God is planning to do something powerful and wonderful, something that will bring even greater glory to his name.

When Lazarus died, Jesus waited to travel to Bethany because he knew he would perform an amazing miracle there, for the glory of God. Many people who witnessed the raising of Lazarus put their faith in Jesus Christ. Over and over, I've seen believers suffer terribly and even die from an illness, yet through it they pointed countless lives toward God's salvation plan.

8. God's Time

Pardon me if this seems blunt, but we all must die (Hebrews 9:27). And, as part of our fallen state, death is often accompanied by sickness and suffering as we leave behind our body of flesh and step into the afterlife.

So, one reason healing may not occur is that it's simply God's time to take a believer home.

In the days surrounding my research and writing of this study on healing, my mother-in-law passed away. Along with my husband and family, we watched her make her journey from earth into eternal life.

Reaching the age of 90, there was a good deal of suffering in her final years, months, weeks and days. But now she is free from pain. She is healed and whole in the presence of our Savior.

Death is the ultimate healing for the believer. And, we have this wonderful promise to look forward to when we reach our destination at home with God in heaven:

> *He will wipe every tear from their eyes, and there will be no more death or sorrow or crying or pain. All these things are gone forever. (Revelation 21:4, NLT)*

CHAPTER 7:
Twelve Healing Oils In The Bible

1. Aloes

Wondering why the cactus-like plant is here? Merriam-Webster has a similar thought, by highlighting aloe first as the tropical plant with a healing gel. But then, the bigger picture emerges: *plural: the fragrant wood of an East Indian tree (Aquilaria agallocha) of the mezereon family*

When the Bible refers to aloes, it's the aromatic extract (or mash) of a tree's heartwood, used for healing and especially embalming. Old English borrowed the word, then applied it to the spiky plant we know now. The Bible lists aloe(s) as:

- *A symbol of abundance and provision (Numbers 24:6)*
- *A perfume (Psalm 45:8, Proverbs 7:17)*
- *An incense (Song of Solomon 4:14)*
- *Burial ointment for Christ (John 19:39)*

While some claim that aloes or aloe wood are the same as sandalwood, the direct connection – A. agallocha – has a powerful essential oil component itself. Used as an incense and cosmetic oil, aloe wood (or eaglewood or agarwood) is known for its benefits as a stimulant and cardiac tonic and can even have some digestive wellness benefits, too! (2)

2. Cassia

Unlike the herb Senna, whose proper name begins with Cassia, the cassia of the Bible resembled our cinnamon more than anything. According to an etymology breakdown by Bible Hub online, cassia is likely *"the inner bark of Cinnamomum cassia, a plant growing in eastern Asia closely allied to that which yields the cinnamon of commerce. It is a fragrant, aromatic bark and was probably used in a powdered form."* (3) The Bible lists cassia as:

- *An anointing oil (Exodus 30:24)*

- *A perfume (Psalm 45:8)*
- *Precious commodities (Ezekiel 27:19)*

Like cinnamon, Cinnamomum cassia is rich in cinnamaldehyde when derived from the bark. (4) If C. cassia is not available, cinnamon essential oil would be a fair switch.

3. Cedarwood

Mentioned most commonly as a burned wood for ceremonial purposes, cedarwood is associated with cleansing and purification. (5) These majestic, ancient trees – likely the cedar of Lebanon (C. libani) – are still around today, and are a source of antioxidant essential oil. According to an analysis of both C. libani and the more commonly used C. atlantica. The Bible lists cedarwood as:

- *A ceremonial tool for cleansing leprosy and (Leviticus 14, Numbers 19)*
- *A perfume (Psalm 45:8)*
- *A symbol of abundance and provision (Numbers 24:6, Psalm 92:12, Ezekiel 31:3)*
- *A symbol of security and stability (Song of Solomon 1:17; 8:9; Zechariah 11:2)*
- *The choice wood for building, trading and currency (referenced by several verses in 2 Samuel, 1 Kings, 2 Kings, 2 Chronicles, Ezra 3, Jeremiah 22, Ezekiel 17)*
- *Mentioned by Solomon in his proverbs and sacred writings (I Kings 4:34)*

There are several uses of cedarwood oil. In the cleansing of the Leper... The oil extracted from the cedars of Lebanon was used to embalm the ancient Pharaohs of Egypt and modern scientists have demonstrated the antioxidant properties of the cedarwood oil. (6)

4. Cypress

Mostly mentioned as a companion to cedar, cypress is celebrated in the Scripture as a symbol of strength and security. One Bible dictionaries states this about Cypress (Hebrew word *Tirzah*):

> *"The Hebrew word is found only in (Isaiah 44:14) We are quite unable to assign any definite rendering to it. The true cypress is a native of the Taurus. The Hebrew word points to some tree with a hard grain, and this is all that can be positively said of it." (7)*

Most modern Bible translations, however, lists cypress several times as:

- *The choice wood for building, trading and currency (referenced by several verses in 1 Kings, 2 Chronicles, Isaiah 41)*

- *A fragrant hardwood and symbol of security & stability (Isaiah 44:14)*

- *A symbol of prosperity (Isaiah 60:13, Hosea 14:8, Zechariah 11:2)*

- *The choice wood for weaponry (Nahum 2:3)*

Cypress is the chosen translation likely due to the Mediterranean cypress (*Cupressus sempervirens*), an evergreen from which we derive an essential oil. Known simply as cypress oil, it is comprised largely of pinene and limonene and is an effective antibacterial essential oil. (8) Whether this is the tree spoken of or anyone burned it for its fragrant release of oil remains to be seen.

5. Frankincense

If you know me at all, you know this is one of favorite oils because of all the research support its used as a natural healer. And if you know the Christmas story, you already know at least one place where frankincense is mentioned in the Bible. Elsewhere, in Exodus 30:34 and Revelation 18:13, frankincense is mentioned as part of incense for a priestly rite and as indication of wealth and prosperity in spice trade. The Bible lists frankincense as:

- *A part of ceremonial offerings (Referenced several times in Leviticus 2, 5, 6, 24; Numbers 5, 1 Chronicles 9, Nehemiah 13)*

- *A holy ceremonial perfume (Exodus 30:34)*

- *A perfume (Song of Solomon 3:6; 4:6)*

- *A precious commodity – potential currency (Isaiah 60:6; Jeremiah 6:20; Revelations 18:13)*

- *The gifts of the Magi to the Christ child (Mathew 2:11)*

As a healing remedy, frankincense oil is not only antimicrobial but also an immunostimulant. (9) Could God have been protecting His priests (and Son!) using frankincense?

6. Galbanum

One of the more unfamiliar of the oils, galbanum was listed in the recipe for incense to be used in the heart of the temple. We don't know the exact species referred to, but we know it was a gum that likely came from a plant in the Ferula family. (10) The Bible lists galbanum as a holy ceremonial perfume (Exodus 30:34)

Today, *Ferula gummosa* is collected and sold as galbanum. It has exhibited antimicrobial effects and potential for use in oral health. (11)

7. Hyssop

The modern hyssop, *Hyssops officinalis*, has been used for antifungal, antibacterial, larvicidal and insect biting deterrent activities. (12) However, according to the International Bible Encyclopedia, this hyssop is not native to the area of Palestine and is not likely to be the oil mentioned throughout the Bible for cleansing and rituals. (13) The Bible lists hyssop as:

- *A part of ritual cleansing and ceremonial offerings (Referenced several times in Exodus 12; Leviticus 14; Numbers 19; Psalm 51; Hebrews 9)*

- *The sponge that soaked up the sour wine that was given to Jesus on the cross (John 19:29)*

- *Mentioned by Solomon in his proverbs and sacred writings (I Kings 4:34)*

While *H. officinalis* does seem to accomplish similar purposes, I personally find it more interesting that the strongest contenders for actual hyssop would be an even closer fit for such purposes: thyme and marjoram.

8. Myrrh

With well documented use throughout the ages, myrrh is easy to identify and enjoy. It by far, the most decorated oil in the Bible being listed as:

- *A precious commodity – potential currency (Genesis 37:25)*

- *Anointing oil (Exodus 30:23)*

- *An ointment (Song of Solomon 5:5)*

- *A perfume (Psalm 45:8, Proverbs 7:17, Song of Solomon 1:13, 4:14, 5:13)*

- *An incense (Song of Solomon 3:6, 4:6)*

- *A with mixed edible spices to be eaten (Song of Solomon 5:1)*

- *The gifts of the Magi to the Christ child (Mathew 2:11)*

- *Mixed with wine and given to Jesus on the cross (Mark 15:23)*

- *Burial preparations Nicodemus used for Jesus' in the tomb (John 19:39)*

Unlike other products from trees, it isn't the wood that is used but the resin that comes from it. Once exposed to air, it hardens and can be powdered, used as-is, or now, distilled for essential oil. Interestingly, myrrh and frankincense essential oils have a synergistic effect when combined, each improving the others' antimicrobial benefits. (14)

9. Myrtle

Myrtle isn't mentioned frequently, but its presence indicates growth and abundance. It likely refers to the *Myrtus communis* plant, which is grown around Jerusalem to this day. (15) The Bible lists myrtle as:

- *The choice wood for building ceremonial booths (Nehemiah 8:15)*
- *A symbol of provision (Isaiah 41:19; 55:13)*
- *A symbol of protection (Zechariah 1:8, 10-11)*

Myrtle is a low growing plant with flowers that produce an intense, lovely aroma. This is said to be the meaning of Esther's Hebrew name – and she would have likely enjoyed her namesake as a perfume in the king's palace! Today, the essential oil specially has undergone a fair amount of research, revealing itself as antimicrobial and an antioxidant, among other benefits. (16)

10. Onycha

Perhaps the most obscure on the list, onycha was mentioned in the holy anointing oil "recipe" and nowhere else. While some sources claim onycha is the resin of the

Styrax benzoin tree, there is little to substantiate the claim. The more commonly accepted view is that it refers to the shell of a mussel, which would have been scraped or powdered and burned. (17) Still others attribute it to balsam or laudanum, a fragrant flowering plant. (18) The Bible lists onycha as a holy ceremonial perfume (Exodus 30:34).

Both Styrax benzoin and Cistus labdanum are developed into essential oils now and can be added to blends and diffused. Neither have been researched thoroughly, though labdanum seems to have good antioxidant capabilities. (19)

11. Rose of Sharon

A rose may not simply be a rose in this case, as the Rose of Sharon is another disputed for its identity. Usually referred to in a metaphorical sense, it could actually refer to any flower that grows well in unfavorable circumstances. (20) It has been said that the "Rose of Sharon" first appeared in the 1611 King James Version of the Bible. The Bible lists Rose of Sharon as a reference to the "Beloved" (Song of Solomon 2:1)

Contenders include a crocus, tulip, or lily, while there are some who contend that it is the Rock Rose, Cistus ladanifer, which is very closely related to labdanum. Without a clear connection and no Biblical "recipe" to indicate ancient use, we are left to imagine the potential of this beautiful, fragrant life during harsh, thorny crags.

12. Spikenard

First introduced in the Old Testament, spikenard is probably most well known as one of the expensive perfumes that the woman anointed Jesus with in Bethany. Spikenard – Narcocracy's jatamansi – was highly prized as a perfume and very precious. It's still used in some beauty treatments to this day. (21) The Bible lists spikenard as:

- *A royal fragrant aroma A symbol (Song of Solomon 1:2)*
- *A prized, desired plant (Song of Solomon 4:13-14)*
- *A costly ointment/perfume used to anoint Christ (Mark 14:3; John 12:3)*

Although there isn't much available yet on the benefits of spikenard (beyond perfumery) as an essential oil, an isolated compound has shown promising effects as an anti-inflammatory. (22)

CHAPTER 8:
Anointing Oil

ANOINTING OIL ALSO referred to as blessing or consecrating oil—is an act that turns standard olive oil into a great spiritual symbol and tool. The process is straightforward, and once the oil is ready, you can use it in a variety of different ways.

Prayer of faith anointing oils for administering to the sick. The Prayer of Faith is James Chapter five verses thirteen thru fifteen:

13 Is anyone among you in trouble? Let them pray. Is anyone happy? Let them sing songs of praise. 14 Is anyone among you sick? Let them call the elders of the church to pray over them and anoint them with oil in the name of the Lord. 15 And the prayer offered in faith will make the sick person well; the Lord will raise them up. If they have sinned, they will be forgiven.

The authority given you for anointing and blessing is found in the book of John Chapter One verses eleven thru thirteen:

11 For the sun rises with scorching heat and withers the plant; its blossom falls, and its beauty is destroyed. In the same way, the rich will fade away even while they go about their business.

12 Blessed is the one who perseveres under trial because, having stood the test, that person will receive the crown of life that the Lord has promised to those who love him.

13 When tempted, no one should say, "God is tempting me." For God cannot be tempted by evil, nor does he tempt anyone. You are a child of God.

Part One - Consecrating the Oil

Oil should be consecrated (blessed) before it is used for anointing. A good quality pure olive oil (scented, if desired, as was done in the early church) should he secured. Those Christian brothers and sisters laboring for the cause of Jesus Christ, standing in his stead, performing. His work on earth, should consecrate it and set it apart for its holy purposes.

- *First hold the open container of oil.*

- *Second address our heavenly father as in prayer.*

- *Third state the authority example "the Lord Jesus Christ".*

- *Fourth consecrate the oil "not the container", setting it apart for the anointing of anyone or anything at any time for any Christian purpose.*

- *Fifth close "in the name of Jesus Christ".*

- *Sixth once the oil is consecrated it is permanent and not necessary to do again.*

An example of a prayer

"Heavenly Father by the authority of the Lord Jesus Christ, I consecrate, dedicate and set apart this special oil for anointing anyone or anything at any time for any Christian purpose, and I do this in the name of "the Lord Jesus Christ Amen".

Part Two - Anointing Use The Words To Modify The Individual Situation

First using a very small amount of oil "draw" a cross on the person forehead or the object that your anointing. Second while applying the oil call the person by their name. Example Brother/ Sister Smith, etc. Third state the authority "the Lord Jesus Christ". Fourth state that you are anointing with this blessed oil. Fifth close in the name of Jesus Christ. An example while applying the oil "Brother/ Sister first name last name", in the name of the Father, The Son, and The Holy Spirit, I anoint you with oil that has been consecrated and set apart for anointing anyone or anything at any time for any Christian purpose and I do this in the name of our Lord Jesus Christ, Amen".

Part Three - Sealing The Anointing/ Blessing

Immediately following the anointing, the Christian brother or sister "and any other Christians present" may lay hands on the head of the person. One of them acts as voice. First "with eyes closed in prayer, call the person by name". Second "state authority the Lord Jesus Christ by which the anointing was performed. Third "seal and confirm the anointing". Fourth "pronounce a blessing as the Holy Spirit dictates". Fifth "close in the name of Jesus Christ".

Note to the administering brother/ sister let the prayer be suited to the situation. It stands to reason prior to visitation the circumstances by pondered. You may even fast for greater spirituality a clearness between you and the Lord, as YOU are the instrument by which God is working through. The leading of a spiritual exemplary life is extremely helpful to you in standing in the Lord's stead.

Part Four - Blessing

Commencing with "brother/ sister first and last name" by the authority of the Lord Jesus Christ. I/ we lay my/our hands upon your head, seal and confirm the anointing and hereby pronounce a blessing upon you/ your life that "the blessing will now be dictated through/ by the Holy Spirit".

It may be long or short, depending on what the spirit has to say. Prayer must proceed from and be accompanied with a lively faith by the person praying and in the person prayed for. Try to instill faith in the person that by his/her faith in the Lord, that healing can and will happen. When the prayer is complete, close in the name of the Lord Jesus Christ.

Types Of Anointing Oils

1. Frankincense and Myrrh

2. Myrrh

3. Rose of Sharon

4. Lily of the valley

5. Spikenard

6. Cedars of Lebanon

7. Balm of Gilead

8. Sweet Cinnamon

9. Oil of Joy/ Gladness

10. Prayer Oil of the Holy Trinity

11. Light of Christ

12. Revelation

13. Exodus

14. Pomegranate

15. Almond

16. Lavender

17. Rainfall

18. Miracle

WOMEN OF THE BIBLE SERIES ANOINTING OILS

1. Mary Mother of Jesus

2. Queen Esther

3. Naomi

4. Ruth

CHAPTER 9:
Procedure For Blessing Anointing Oil

Part One -Check with your judicatory or a religious authority for specifics.

Each denomination has its own guidelines governing the way that oil is blessed for anointing purposes, as well as the way that anointing oil is used.

- *The most common restriction regards who may bless or anoint the oil. In some denominations, only a priest or similar clergyman can bless the oil. Some denominations even limit which clergymen are authorized to consecrate oil.*

- *It is also important to note that some denominations also have guidelines and laws concerning how the oil should be consecrated and how it can be used afterward.*

- *Other possible rules may include those governing how the oil is obtained and the oil you can use.*

-

Part Two - Obtain olive oil

You can use plain or scented olive oil, but it should be olive oil either way

- *Unless you are told otherwise by a religious authority, it is not necessary to buy special oil for anointing.*

- *Extra-virgin cold-pressed olive oil is the purest variety available, so many people prefer to use that when shopping for an anointing oil. You can find this oil in most of grocery stores.*

- *If desired, you can buy scented olive oil from a religious or secular store. Oil that has been perfumed with frankincense and myrrh is both popular and spiritually significant.*

Part three - Place a small amount of oil in a vial.

Find a small vial, bottle, or other container with a tight lid that does not leak. Pour a little olive oil into this container. The sample in this container will become the anointing oil.

- *You can buy a special oil stock at a religious bookstore or online, or you could use any small bottle.*

- *The most common vial is a short metal container with a screw-on lid, with a sponge placed inside to help hold the oil in.*

- *Less expensive plastic oil stocks are also available.*

- *Even a "travel size" plastic shampoo bottle could be used.*

Part Four - Pray a blessing over the oil

If your denomination does not prohibit it, you can usually pray a blessing over the oil on your own and without the help of a religious authority figure. The prayer should be firm, and one made in full faith.

- *The prayer you use must ask God to bless and cleanse the oil, so that it can be used for the sake of God's glory.*

- *For instance, the prayer might be something like, "God, I pray that you anoint this oil in Your heavenly name. I pray that You cleanse it of any defilement in it or upon it, and that You make it holy for the work of Your glory. May this be done in the name of the Father, the Son, and the Holy Spirit. Amen."[3]*

Part Five - Store the oil at room temperature

The best way to keep the oil fresh is to store it sealed and at room temperature. Refrigeration is not recommended.

- *If you refrigerate the oil, it will start to look cloudy. This is not harmful, though, and the oil can still be used even if it has gotten cloudy.*

CHAPTER 10:
Using Anointing Oil

Part One - Understand

the true power behind anointing oil

There is nothing mystical or magical about the oil itself, even though anointing oil can be a powerful tool of the faith. As with all other spiritual tools, the real power comes from God.

- *Anointing oil is a symbol of your faith in God and of God's ability to cleanse and make things holy.*

- *Without faith, anointing oil will not have any positive effect. You can use oil to help strengthen and demonstrate your faith, but you cannot use it to replace faith.*

Part Two: Anoint yourself.

Among other things, you can use the oil to anoint yourself when you pray, when you are troubled, or when you are sick.

- *While there are different ways to anoint yourself, the most common is to wet your right thumb with a little of the oil and make a Sign of the Cross on your forehead; draw a cross on your forehead while saying, "In the name of the Father, and of the Son, and of the Holy Spirit. Amen."*

- *After anointing yourself, you can continue with your prayers as you usually would, regardless of whether it is a prayer for healing, repentance, thanksgiving, or anything else.*

- *Alternatively, if you are injured or ill, you could cross yourself with the anointing oil over the damaged area of your body while praying for healing.*

Part Three: Anoint others

Just as you can use the anointing oil on yourself, you can also use it to aid others who are troubled or ill. Pray over the other person as you anoint them with the oil.

- *When anointing someone else, wet your right thumb with a little of the anointing oil and use it to draw a cross in the middle of the other person's forehead.*

- *As you draw the cross, state the person's name and state, "I anoint you with oil in the name of the Father, and of the Son, and of the Holy Spirit."*

- *Follow this with any prayers that are appropriate to the specific circumstances. This includes prayers for physical healing, spiritual healing, consecration, and general blessing.*

Part Four: Use anointing oil in your home

Anointing oil is commonly used when blessing a new home or a home that has faced some form of spiritual threat.

- *Remove anything from the home that may have any evil roots.*

- *Walk around your home anointing the frame of every door in every room. As you anoint each frame, pray that God fills your house with the Holy Spirit, and that everything that happens in the house will be done in according to God's will.*

- *The idea behind anointing your home is that you are turning it into "holy ground" for God.*

Part Five: Note a few traditional uses

Anointing oil has roots that date back to biblical times. While some of the more traditional uses are rarely applied nowadays, it is still worth noting what some of those uses were.

- *Anointing the body with perfumed oil was once used to refresh the body. If done to someone else, the act was considered one of hospitality.*

- *The Ancient Israelites once rubbed consecrated oil on the leather of their shields to prepare for war.*

- *Some anointing oils were used for medicinal purposes, while others were used to prepare bodies for funerals and burials.*

- *Some oils were also used to purify the body or consecrate an individual for a specific purpose or calling within God's plan.*

CHAPTER 11:
Forty Scriptures About Anointing Oil

1. **James 5:14**

   Is anyone among you sick? Then he must call for the elders of the church and they are to pray over him, anointing him with oil in the name of the Lord;

2. **Exodus 29:7**

   "Then you shall take the anointing oil and pour it on his head and anoint him.

3. **Mark 6:13**

   And they were casting out many demons and were anointing with oil many sick people and healing them.

4. **Hebrews 1:9**

   You have loved righteousness and hated lawlessness; therefore god, your god, has anointed you with the oil of gladness above your companions.

5. **Ruth 3:3**

   Wash yourself therefore, and anoint yourself and put on your best clothes, and go down to the threshing floor; but do not make yourself known to the man until he has finished eating and drinking.

6. **Isaiah 61:1**

   The Spirit of the Lord GOD is upon me, Because the LORD has anointed me to bring good news to the afflicted; He has sent me to bind up the brokenhearted, to proclaim liberty to captives and freedom to prisoners;

7. **Luke 7:46**

   You did not anoint My head with oil, but she anointed My feet with perfume.

8. **Psalm 45:7**

   You have loved righteousness and hated wickedness; Therefore God, Your God, has anointed You With the oil of joy above Your fellows.

9. **1 John 2:27**

   As for you, the anointing which you received from Him abides in you, and you have no need for anyone to teach you; but as His anointing teaches you about all things, and is true and is not a lie, and just as it has taught you, you abide in Him.

10. **Luke 10:34**

    and came to him and bandaged up his wounds, pouring oil and wine on them; and he put him on his own beast, and brought him to an inn and took care of him.

11. **2 Samuel 14:2**

So, Joab sent to Tekoa and brought a wise woman from there and said to her, "Please pretend to be a mourner, and put on mourning garments now, and do not anoint yourself with oil, but be like a woman who has been mourning for the dead many days;

12. **Leviticus 8:12**

Then he poured some of the anointing oil on Aaron's head and anointed him, to consecrate him.

13. **Exodus 25:6**

oil for lighting, spices for the anointing oil and for the fragrant incense,

14. **1 Samuel 16:13**

Then Samuel took the horn of oil and anointed him in the midst of his brothers; and the Spirit of the LORD came mightily upon David from that day forward. And Samuel arose and went to Ramah.

15. **Psalm 23:5**

You prepare a table before me in the presence of my enemies; You have anointed my head with oil; My cup overflows.

16. **Daniel 10:3**

I did not eat any tasty food, nor did meat or wine enter my mouth, nor did I use any ointment at all until the entire three weeks were completed.

17. **Mark 14:8**

She has done what she could; she has anointed My body beforehand for the burial.

18. **Isaiah 21:5**

They set the table, they spread out the cloth, they eat, they drink; "Rise up, captains, oil the shields,"

19. **Exodus 28:41**

You shall put them on Aaron your brother and on his sons with him; and you shall anoint them and ordain them and consecrate them, that they may serve Me as priests.

20. **Exodus 40:9**

Then you shall take the anointing oil and anoint the tabernacle and all that is in it, and shall consecrate it and all its furnishings; and it shall be holy.

21. **Luke 7:38**

And standing behind Him at His feet, weeping, she began to wet His feet with her tears, and kept wiping them with the hair of her head, and kissing His feet and anointing them with the perfume.

22. **James 5:14-16**

Is anyone among you sick? Then he must call for the elders of the church and they are to pray over him, anointing him with oil in the name of the Lord; and the prayer offered in faith will restore the one who is sick, and the Lord will raise him up, and if he has committed sins, they will be forgiven him. Therefore, confess your sins to one another, and pray for one another so that you may be healed the effective prayer of a righteous man can accomplish much.

23. **Psalm 92:10**

But You have exalted my horn like that of the wild ox; I have been anointed with fresh oil.

24. **Exodus 30:30**

You shall anoint Aaron and his sons, and consecrate them, that they may minister as priests to Me.

25. **Leviticus 8:30**

So, Moses took some of the anointing oil and some of the blood which was on the altar and sprinkled it on Aaron, on his garments, on his sons, and on the garments of his sons with him; and he consecrated Aaron, his garments, and his sons, and the garments of his sons with him.

26. **Isaiah 10:27**

So, it will be in that day, that his burden will be removed from your shoulders and his yoke from your neck, and the yoke will be broken because of fatness.

27. Acts 18:28

For he powerfully refuted the Jews in public, demonstrating by the Scriptures that Jesus was the Christ.

28. Genesis 28:18

So, Jacob rose early in the morning, and took the stone that he had put under his head and set it up as a pillar and poured oil on its top.

29. Acts 10:38

You know of Jesus of Nazareth, how God anointed Him with the Holy Spirit and with power, and how He went about doing good and healing all who were oppressed by the devil, for God was with Him.

30. Exodus 30:31

You shall speak to the sons of Israel, saying, 'This shall be a holy anointing oil to Me throughout your generations.

31. **Deuteronomy 28:40**

You shall have olive trees throughout your territory, but you will not anoint yourself with the oil, for your olives will drop off.

32. **Psalm 45:8**

All Your garments are fragrant with myrrh and aloes and cassia; Out of ivory palaces stringed instruments have made You glad.

33. **John 12:3**

Mary then took a pound of very costly perfume of pure nard, and anointed the feet of Jesus and wiped His feet with her hair; and the house was filled with the fragrance of the perfume.

34. **Exodus 35:28**

And the spice and the oil for the light and for the anointing oil and for the fragrant incense.

35. **Isaiah 61:3**

To grant those who mourn in Zion, giving them a garland instead of ashes, the oil of gladness instead of mourning, the mantle of praise instead of a spirit of fainting So they will be called oaks of righteousness, the planting of the LORD, that He may be glorified.

36. **Psalm 133:2**

It is like the precious oil upon the head, coming down upon the beard, Even Aaron's beard, Coming down upon the edge of his robes.

37. **Exodus 30:25**

You shall make of these a holy anointing oil, a perfume mixture, the work of a perfumer; it shall be a holy anointing oil.

38. **Matthew 6:17**

But you, when you fast, anoint your head and wash your face

39. **Exodus 30:31-32**

You shall speak to the sons of Israel, saying, 'This shall be a holy anointing oil to Me throughout your generations. 'It shall not be poured on anyone's body, nor shall you make any like it in the same proportions; it is holy, and it shall be holy to you.

40. Exodus 30:26-29

With it you shall anoint the tent of meeting and the ark of the testimony, and the table and all its utensils, and the lampstand and its utensils, and the altar of incense, and the altar of burnt offering and all its utensils, and the laver and its stand.

CHAPTER 12:
Forgiveness and Love Scriptures

The importance of these scriptures in bringing about divine healing should not be underestimated. These scriptures are the cornerstone of healing

1. **James 5:16**

    Therefore, confess your sins to each other and pray for each other so that you may be healed. The prayer of a righteous man is powerful and effective

2. **Hebrews 13:1-2**

   Keep on loving each other as brothers. Do not forget to entertain strangers, for by so doing some people have entertained angels without knowing it

3. **John 15:12-14**

   My command is this: love each other as I have loved you. Greater love has no one than this, that he lay down his life for his friends. You are my friends if you do what I command

4. **1 Corinthians 13:4-7**

   Love is patient, love is kind. It does not envy, it does not boast it is not proud. It is not rude, it is not self-seeking, it is not easily angered, it keeps no record of wrongs. Love does not delight in evil but rejoices with the truth. It always protects, always trusts, always hopes, always perseveres

5. **Proverbs 15:30**

   A cheerful look brings joy to the heart, and good news gives health to the bones

6. **Proverbs 12:18**

   Reckless words pierce like a sword but the tongue of the wise brings healing

7. **Proverbs 16:24**

   Pleasant words are a honeycomb, sweet to the soul and healing to the bones

8. **Isaiah 58:7-8**

   Is it not to share your food with the hungry and to provide the poor wanderer with shelter when you see the naked, to clothe him, and not to turn away from your own flesh and blood? Then your light will break forth like the dawn, and your healing will quickly appear, then your righteousness will go before you and the glory of the Lord will be your rear guard

9. **Romans 13:9-10**

   The commandments, "Do not commit adultery", "Do not murder", "Do not steal", "Do not covet" and whatever other commandment there may be, are summed up in this one rule: "love your neighbor as yourself". Love does not harm to its neighbor. Therefore, love is the fulfillment of the law.

10. **Mark 11:23-25**

   "I tell you the truth, if anyone says to this mountain, "Go, throw yourself into the sea', and does not doubt in his heart but believes that what he says will happen, it will be done for him. Therefore, I tell you, whatever you ask for in prayer believe that you have received it, and it will be yours. And when you stand praying, if you hold anything against anyone, forgive him, so that your father in heaven may forgive you your sins.

11. John 14:23

Jesus replied, "if anyone loves me, he will obey my teaching. My father will love him, and we will come to him and make our home with him

CHAPTER 13:
Healing Foods, Scriptures And Your Diet

1. **Apples**

    Song of Solomon 2:5

    Strengthen me with raisins, refresh me with apples, for I am faint with love.

2. **Barley**

    Deuteronomy 8:7-9

    For the Lord your God is bringing you into a good land---land with streams and pools of water, with spring flowing in the valleys and hills; a land with wheat and barley, vines and fig trees, pomegranates, olive and honey; a land where bread will not be scarce, and you lack nothing; a land where the rocks are iron, and you can dig copper out of the hills

3. Beans

Ezekiel 4:9

Take wheat and barley, beans, lentils, millet and spelt; put them in a storage jar and use them to make bread for yourself. You are to eat it during the 390 days you lie on your side.

2 Samuel 17:28-29

Brought bedding and bowls and articles of pottery. They also brought wheat and barley, flour and roasted grain, beans, and lentils, honey and curds, sheep and cheese from cow's milk for David and his people to eat. For they said, "The people have become hungry and tired and thirsty in the desert".

4. Bread

Ezekiel 4:9

"Take wheat and barley, beans and lentils, millet and spelt; put them in a storage jar and use them to make bread for yourself. You are to eat it during the 390 days you lie on your side.

5. Dairy

Isaiah 7:15

He will eat curds and honey when he knows enough to reject the wrong and choose the right.

Isaiah 7:22

And because of the abundance of the milk they give, he will have curds to eat. All who remain in the land will eat curds and honey.

Proverbs 27:27

You will have plenty of goat's milk to feed you and your family and to nourish your servant girls.

6. Figs

1 Samuel 30:11-12

They found an Egyptian in a field and brought him to David. They gave him water to drink and food to eat—part of a cake of pressed figs and two cakes of raisins. He ate and was revived, for he had not eaten any food or drunk any water for three days and three nights.

7. Fish

Leviticus 11:9-12

Of all the creatures living in the water of the seas and the streams, you may eat any that have fins and scales. But all creatures in the seas or streams that do not have fins and scales whether among all the swarming things or among all the other living creatures in the water—you are to detest. And since you are to detest them, you must not eat their meat and you must detest their carcasses. Anything living in the water that does not have fins and scales is to be detestable to you.

Deuteronomy 14:9

Of all the creatures living in the water, you may eat any that has fins and scales.

Luke 24:42-43

They gave him a piece of broiled fish and he took it and ate it in their presence

8. Fruit

Ezekiel 47:12

Fruit trees of all kinds will grow on both banks of the river. Their leaves will not wither, nor will their fruit fail. Every month they will bear, because the water from the sanctuary flows to them. Their fruit will serve food and their leaves for healing

Deuteronomy 8:7

For the Lord your God is bringing you into a good land—a land with streams and pools of water, with springs flowing in the valleys and hills; a land with wheat and barley, vines and fig trees, pomegranates, olive oil and honey; a land where bread will not be scarce, and you will lack nothing; a land where they rocks are iron and you can dig copper out of the hills.

Song of Solomon 2:5

Strengthen me with raisins, refresh me with apples, for I am faint with love

9. Garlic

Numbers 11:5

We remember the fish we ate in Egypt at no cost also the cucumbers, melons, leeks, onions and garlic

10. Grains

Ezekiel 4:9

Take wheat and barley, beans and lentils, millet and spelt; put them in a storage jar and use them to make bread for yourself. You are to eat it during the three hundred ninety days you lie on your side

11. Grapes

Numbers 13:23

When they reached the Valley of Eschol, they cut off a branch bearing a single cluster of grapes. Two of them carried it on a pole between them, along with some pomegranates and figs.

Genesis 9:20

Noah, a man of the soil, proceeded to plant a vineyard

1 Timothy 5:23

Stop drinking only water and use a little wine because of your stomach and your frequent illnesses

1 Kings 21:2

Ahab said to Naboth, "Let me have your vineyard to use for a vegetable garden, since it is close to my palace. In exchange I will give you a better

vineyard or if you prefer, I will pay you whatever it
is worth"

12. Herbs

Numbers 11:7-9

The manna was like coriander seed and looked like
resin. The people went around gathering it and
then ground it in a hand mill or crushed it in a
mortar. They cooked it in a pot or made it into
cakes. And it tasted like something made with
olive oil. When the dew settled on the camp at
night, the manna also came down.

Psalm 51:7

Cleanse me with hyssop and I will be clean; wash
me and I will be whiter than snow

John 19:29-30

A jar of wine vinegar was there so they soaked a
sponge in it, put the sponge on a stalk of the
hyssop plant, and lifted it to Jesus lips. When he
had received the drink, Jesus said, "It is finished".
With that, he bowed his head and gave up his
spirit

13. Honey

1 Samuel 14:27

But Jonathan had not heard that his father had bound the people with the oath, so he reached out the end of the staff that was in his hand and dipped it into the honeycomb. He raised his hand to his mouth and his eyes brightened

2 Samuel 17:29

Honey and curds, sheep and cheese from cow's milk for David and his people to eat. For they said, "The people have become hungry and tired and thirsty in the desert".

Genesis 43:11

Then their father Israel said to them, "if it must be, then do this: put some of the best products of the land in your bags and take them down to the man as a gift—a little balm and a little honey, some spices and myrrh, some pistachio nuts and almonds

14. Meat

Genesis 9:3

Everything that lives, and moves will be food for you. Just as I gave you the green plants, I now gibe you everything

Leviticus 7:22-27

The Lord said to Moses, "say to the Israelites: Do not eat any of the fat of cattle, sheep or goats. The fat of an animal found dead or torn by wild animals may be used for any other purpose, but you must not eat it. Anyone who eats the fat of an animal from which an offering by fire may be made to the Lord must be cut off from his people. And wherever you live, you must not eat the blood of any bird or animal. If anyone eats blood that person must be cut off from his people"

Leviticus 3:17

This is a lasting ordinance for the generations to come, wherever you live. You must not eat any fat or any blood

15. Melon

Numbers 11:5

We remember the fish we ate in Egypt at no cost also the cucumbers, melons, leeks, onions and garlic

Isaiah 1:8

The daughter of Zion is left like a shelter in a vineyard, like a hut in a field of melons, like a city under siege

16. Milk

Exodus 3:8

So, I have come down to rescue them from the hand of the Egyptians and to bring them up out of that land into a good and spacious land, a land flowing with milk and honey—the home of the Canaanites, Hittites, Amorites, Perizzites, Hivites and Jebusites

Isaiah 7:22

And because of the abundance of the milk they give, he will have curds to eat. All who remain in the land will eat curds and honey.

2 Samuel 17:29

Honey and curds, sheep and cheese from cow's milk for David and his people to eat. For they said, "the people have become hungry and tired and thirsty in the desert"

17. Nuts

Genesis 43:11

Then their father Israel said to them, "if it must be then do this: put some of the best products of the land in your bags and take them down to the man as a gift—a little balm and a little honey, some spices and myrrh, some pistachio nuts and almonds

18. Olives

James 5:14

Is anyone of you sick? He should call the elders of the church to pray over him and anoint him with oil in the name of the Lord.

2 Kings 18:32

Until I come and take you to a land like your own, a land a grain and new wine, a land of bread and vineyards, a land of olive trees and honey. Choose life and not death! "Do not listen to Hezekiah, for he is misleading you when he says, the Lord will deliver us"

19. Onions

Numbers 11:5

We remember the fish we ate in Egypt at no cost—also the cucumbers, melons, leeks, onions and garlic

20. Pomegranates

Deuteronomy 8:8

A land with wheat and barley, vines and fig trees, pomegranates, olive oil and honey

21. Spices

Matthew 23:23

"Woe to you, teachers of the law and Pharisees, you hypocrites! You give a tenth of your spices mint, dill and cumin. But you have neglected the more important matters of the law, justice, mercy and faithfulness. You should have practiced the latter, without neglecting the former

Luke 11:42

"Woe to you Pharisees because you give God a tenth of your mint, rue and all other kinds of garden herbs, but you neglect justice and the love of God. You should have practiced the latter without leaving the former undone"

22. Vegetables

Daniel 1:12-17

"Please test your servants for ten days: Give us nothing but vegetables to eat and water to drink. Then compare our appearance with that of the young men who eat the royal food and treat your servants in accordance with what you see". So, he agreed to this and tested them for ten days. At the end of the ten days they looked healthier and better nourished than any of the young men who ate the royal food. So, the guard took away their choice food and the wine they were to drink and gave them vegetables instead. To these four young men God gave knowledge and understanding of all kinds of literature and learning. And Daniel could understand visions and dreams of all kinds

Numbers 11:5

We remember the fish we ate in Egypt at no cost also the cucumbers, melons, leeks, onions and garlic

Ezekiel 4:9

"Take wheat and barley, beans and lentils, millet and spelt; put them in a storage jar and use them to make bread for yourself. You are to eat it during the three hundred and ninety days you lie on your side

Genesis 1:11

Then God said, "Let the land produce vegetation: seed-bearing plants and trees on the face of the whole earth and every tree that has fruit with seed in it. They will be yours for food

23. Wheat

Jeremiah 41:8

But ten of them said to Ishmael, "Don't kill us! We have wheat and barley, oil and honey, hidden in a field". So, he let them alone and did not kill them with the others

Ezekiel 4:9

"Take wheat and barley, beans and lentils, millet and spelt; put them in a storage jar and use them to make bread for yourself. You are to eat it during the three hundred ninety days you lie on your side

24. Yogurt (Curds)

2 Samuel 17:28-29

Brought bedding and bowls and articles of pottery. They also brought wheat and barley, flour and roasted grain, beans and lentils, honey and curds, sheep, and cheese from cow's milk for David and his people to eat. For they said, "The people have become hungry and tired and thirsty in the dessert"

CHAPTER 14:
Healing Miracles Of Jesus In The Gospel

1. Official's dying son
2. Madman in the synagogue
3. Peter's mother in-law's fever
4. Jesus continues healing
5. The Leper
6. Paralyzed man
7. Invalid at the pool of Bethesda
8. The man with the shriveled hand
9. Jesus continues healing many

10. Roman centurion's servant

11. The widow of Nain's dead son

12. Dumb and blind man

13. Madman and the Gadarene pigs

14. Woman with the hemorrhage

15. Raising of Jairus' daughter

16. Two blind men and the dumb man

17. Jesus heals the sick at Gennesaret

18. Deaf of Syrophoenician woman

19. Deaf and dumb in Decapolis

20. Blind man of Bethsaida

21. Epileptic boy

22. Ten lepers

23. The man born blind

24. Crippled woman

25. The man with dropsy

26. Lazarus raised from the dead

27. Blind man or men near Jericho

Printed in Great Britain
by Amazon